I N HIS LETTER introducing his proposal for revamping the Elementary and Secondary Education Act, otherwise known as the No Child Left Behind law, President Barack Obama said he was presenting an "outline for a re-envisioned federal role in education." Although he acknowledged that "we must recognize the importance of communities and families in supporting their children's education, because a parent is a child's first teacher," Obama's key education policies have disempowered local communities and parents and centralized education policy and decision making in Washington.

Unlike Obama's well-known and much-discussed health care policies, many Americans are unfamiliar with either the broad themes or the details of President Obama's education policies. There is some awareness, however, that the president has increased federal spending on education through, for ex - ample, his stimulus plan, the 2009 American Recovery and Reinvestment Act (ARRA).

Under ARRA, nearly two times the annual

budget of the federal Department of Education (USDE) – about $100 billion – was allocated to improve the nation's public school system. Arne Duncan, Obama's education secretary, called this one-time allocation "absolutely a once-in-a-lifetime opportunity to lift American education to a new level – and make us more competitive in the global economy." Compared with such high-flown rhetoric, the results of this huge federal education spending spree were a bitter disappointment.

The U.S. Government Accountability Office found that instead of funding reforms and raising student achievement, the education-stimulus money simply went to "retaining staff and current education programs" – i.e., preserving the status quo. Other analyses of ARRA education funding have come to similar conclusions. Yet despite this massive failure, the administration's most far-reaching and troubling education program cost a fraction of ARRA's overall price tag.

Initially funded at $4.35 billion, Race to the

Top (RTTT) is a federal competitive grant program that was a small part of the bigger ARRA allocation. In their grant applications, states had to address issues such as how they would increase teacher effectiveness, build data systems to measure student success, and turn around low-performing schools. However, it was the important extra points given to states that agreed to adopt common, or national, academic and college-and-career-readiness standards and assessments that raised a large red flag for anyone concerned about the potential nationalization of American education.

THE NATIONAL STANDARDS

Obama, Duncan, and other supporters of national academic-content standards argue that a single set of rigorous national standards and a single national test aligned with them are needed because the current system of individual state standards and tests has given the country a hodgepodge of standards of differing quality. Duncan has stated, "If we accomplish one thing in the coming years, it should be to eliminate the extreme variation in standards across America." In order to accomplish this goal, Duncan and the president have chosen a strategy of unprecedented federal activism.

The New York Times has observed that Duncan "has far more money to dole out than any previous secretary of education, and he is using it in ways that extend the federal government's reach into virtually every area of education, from pre-kindergarten to college." Yet the Obama administration has tried to be stealthy about its activist and intrusive agenda.

Knowing that creating national standards inside the U.S. Department of Education would never fly, the administration decided to use a third-party product. The National Governors Association and the Council of Chief State School Officers, both influential Washington-based organizations, collaborated to create the so-called Common Core standards. These sub-

> *The Obama administration has tried to be stealthy about its activist and intrusive agenda.*

ject-matter and college-and-career-readiness standards were then used as de facto national standards by the Obama administration.

Texas Commissioner of Education Robert Scott condemned this stalking-horse tactic: "Having the federal government use Washington-based special interest groups and vendors as proxy for the USDE in setting national curriculum standards and then using ARRA federal discretionary funds to develop national tests for every child in the nation represents unprecedented intrusiveness by the federal government into the personal lives of our children and their families."

States had to sign on to these Common Core national standards to earn critical points under Race to the Top, and these standards are emphasized in President Obama's blueprint for reauthorization of the Elementary and Secondary Education Act. In addition, in early 2011, the president told the nation's governors that he wanted states to adopt national standards as a precondition for receiving federal Title I funding for disadvantaged students.

To further camouflage its intentions, the Obama administration has constantly claimed that the Common Core standards are voluntary and are not mandated by the federal government. The administration argues that states could have chosen not to participate in Race to the Top and thus would not be subject to any national standards and testing. Both conservatives and liberals find this line of reasoning singularly unconvincing.

Andy Smarick, a former U.S. deputy assistant secretary of education under President George W. Bush, observed that "because states are still desperate for money, it's doubtful that they will take a pass on the opportunity to compete for several hundred million dollars."

From the Left, Anthony Cody, a liberal-leaning blogger for *Education Week* and a former teacher, writes, "In today's fiscal climate, when state revenues have declined drastically, federal funding has become an absolute necessity. Though states and local districts technically have the option of refusing these funds, in practice they are totally dependent on them." Eventually, "we may end with all of our states 'volunteering' to become centralized, with the [federal] Department of Education ... at the helm."

Not surprisingly, most states, with the exception of Texas and a few others, agreed to the Common Core national standards in their RTTT applications. As one Wisconsin state legislator opined, "This is a race for the money, not a race for the top."

Texas Education Commissioner Scott harshly assessed the Obama administration's stealth nationalization policies: "Originally sold to the states as voluntary, states have now been told that participation in national standards and national testing would be required as a condition of receiving federal

[7]

discretionary grant funding under the American Recovery and Reinvestment Act administered by the USDE. The effort has now become a cornerstone of the Administration's education policy through the USDE's prioritization of adoption of national standards and aligned national tests in receiving federal funds."

The ultimate goal of President Obama's national-standards-and-testing drive, Scott warned, is nothing less than the "federal takeover of the nation's public schools." Such a power grab, based on national standards and testing, would have terrible educational and governance consequences for America.

The Cost of National Standards

Although they may have qualms about accepting national standards and testing, most revenue-starved states leaped at the chance to reel in more federal education bucks. Yet state lawmakers and officials may have made a huge fiscal miscalculation. While states were rushing headlong into the RTTT competition and its programmatic requirements, there were voices in the wilderness warning of the enormous cost of changing over to the new national-standards-and-testing system.

"The Common Core standards would further burden already overstrained state budgets," said Lindsey Burke, education-policy analyst at The Heritage Foundation. "Developing and overhauling state accountability systems," she warned, "will be far more costly and of questionable value during a time of budget shortfalls nationwide."

Although they may have qualms about accepting national standards and testing, most revenue-starved states leaped at the chance to reel in more federal education bucks.

Frederick Hess, education policy director at the American Enterprise Institute, observes that "most state policymakers – who have been busy slashing outlays and who are eyeballing several tough budget cycles ahead – have no idea that supporting Common Core standards means that they're signing up for large new outlays for implementation and assessment."

"At this point the national standards are just a bunch of words on pieces of paper," observes Jay Greene, head of the Department of Education Reform at the University of Arkansas. He explains, "To make standards meaningful they have to be integrated with changes in curriculum, assessment, and pedagogy. Changing all that will take a ton of money since it involves changing textbooks, tests, professional development, teacher training, etc." For most states, these costs come at a time when they can least afford them.

California had one of the nation's top sets of state academic-content standards. Yet, bedeviled by massive, continuing budget deficits, the state decided to replace its high-rated state standards with the Common Core national standards when it applied for RTTT funding. Like most other states, California was a loser in the RTTT sweepstakes but is now saddled with the costly prospect of overhauling its standards-and-testing system.

The California Department of Education estimates that it will cost $759 million to im -plement the national standards. However, EdSource, a respected Northern California-based education-research organization, estimates that it will cost $800 million for new curriculum frameworks and $785 million for teacher and principal training, plus various costs for other items, resulting in a total of $1.6 billion to change over to the new national standards.

Doug Lasken, a consultant on state standards and a former teacher, noted that California's slice of the RTTT money, if it won a grant, was estimated to be about $400 million, "though little of that money would have been dedicated to [Common Core standards] adoption costs." He rightly wondered how such an amount "could cover an expense of $1.6 billion." Because California lost its bid for RTTT funding, Lasken lamented, "We will, therefore, receive no federal money to cover the expense of replacing our standards."

A report by the Superintendent of Public Instruction's Office in Washington State found that the cost just to buy new textbooks that align with the new national standards would be $122 million. Liv Finne, director of education at the Washington Policy Center, says that when all costs – including those to update the state's testing system – are totaled, the amount exceeds $300 million. And, like California, Washington State failed to win an RTTT grant.

The Obama administration admits that the costs of implementing the new national standards and tests are very high. *Education Week* reported that Roberto Rodriguez, a key White House education adviser, "acknowledged that the cost of [teacher] professional development necessary to make common standards and assessments work the way they should is 'huge.'" While he said the administration was "looking into" ways to help states with these costs, his vagueness makes it clear that Barack Obama and Arne Duncan have no real, concrete strategy to assist states with funding the full implementation of the national standards and tests.

THE NATIONAL STANDARDS ARE NOT HIGH STANDARDS

Obama-administration officials may concede that the states will have to bear significant costs, but they and their allies would likely retort that the price is worth it because the new national standards are much better than the current crop of state standards. The creators of Common Core, for example, claim their standards "are evidence-based, aligned with college and work expectations, include rigorous content and skills, and are informed by other top performing countries." The evidence, however, fails to bear out this boast.

Various studies have been done comparing

the rigor of the Common Core national standards with the state standards that they will replace. For national-standards advocates, the findings are disappointing.

A University of Pennsylvania study conducted by Andrew Porter, dean of the university's graduate school of education, and several research colleagues compared the national math standards with 27 state math standards. They also compared the national English language arts standards with 24 state English standards. According to Porter, "What we found was unexpected and troubling."

"Our research shows that the common-core standards do not represent a meaningful improvement over existing state standards," says Porter. He points out that "in terms of mathematics and English language arts curricula focus, the results are just as disappointing: The common core has a greater focus than certain state standards, and a lesser focus than others."

"What all this means is that the common-core standards don't seem to build on what we've learned through decades of research and experience," Porter concludes. "The common core is not a new gold standard – it's firmly in the middle of the pack of current curricula."

President Obama has said, "We will not be able to keep the American promise of equal opportunity if we fail to provide a world-class education to every child." The national standards promoted by the president are supposed to help deliver that world-class education. The University of Pennsylvania study, however, also questioned the quality of the Common Core national standards compared with the standards of top-performing countries such as Finland, Japan, and New Zealand. It found that the standards in these countries put more emphasis on basic skills than the Common Core standards did. This does not bode well for the U.S., where large percentages of students entering college require remedial instruction in basic math and English.

In their paper, Porter and his colleagues warn, "If the new standards don't bring us better curricula than we already have, don't help us catch up with our international competitors, and don't lead to better assessments, then all the hoopla over the common core may turn out to be much ado about nothing."

James Milgram, professor emeritus of mathematics at Stanford University, was a member of the Validation Committee for the Common Core national standards and, shockingly, was the only math-content expert on the 25-member committee. In that capacity, he reviewed the national math standards and gave a big thumbs-down on their quality. The national standards, he charges, are a product of politics, rather than an objective focus on what works best for children.

Testifying before a committee of the Texas Legislature, Milgram said, "As a result of all the political pressure to make [Common] Core Standards acceptable to the special-interest groups involved, there are a number of ex-tremely problematic decisions that were made in writing them." These special interests "were mainly focused on things like making the standards as non-challenging as possible."

Regarding geometry, Milgram noted that "the most likely outcome of the [Common] Core Mathematics geometry standards is the complete suppression of the key topics in Euclidean geometry, including proofs and deductive reasoning." Such shortcomings mean that America's new national math standards do not stack up well against the foreign competition.

"For example," Milgram told Texas lawmakers, "by the end of the fifth grade, the material being covered in arithmetic and algebra in [Common] Core Standards is more than a year behind the early grade expectations in most high-achieving countries." Further, "by the end of the seventh grade, [Common] Core Standards are roughly two years behind."

Milgram scathingly concluded, "The [Common] Core Mathematics Standards are written to reflect very low expectations. More exactly, the explicitly stated objective is to prepare students not to have to take remedial mathematics courses at a typical community college." Not exactly the world-class education benchmark that President Obama says is needed to help American students compete in the global marketplace.

For states that had higher subject-matter standards than the new national standards, the future prospects for their school systems and their students are especially dim.

In a study for the Boston-based Pioneer Institute, Sandra Stotsky, professor of education reform at the University of Arkansas and member of the Validation Committee for the Common Core national standards, and Ze'ev Wurman, former senior policy adviser at the U.S. Department of Education and a top standards expert, found that the new national standards were significantly inferior to the high state standards in California and Massachusetts.

Stotsky and Wurman found that "overall, Common Core's preparation for Algebra I falls a year or two behind the standards in California." Specifically, California's standards prepare all students to take Algebra I in the eighth grade. All high-achieving countries have a similar Algebra I requirement. In contrast, the Common Core national standards "aim for little more than pre-algebra in grade 8."

Not requiring Algebra I before high school will likely have a significant impact on student achievement, since data show that high school

---

The Obama administration admits that the costs of implementing the new national standards and tests are very high.

---

freshmen whose first high school math course was geometry scored much higher on the National Assessment of Educational Progress math exam than freshmen whose first math course was Algebra I.

In English language arts, Stotsky and Wurman found that by adopting the new national standards, "California and Massachusetts significantly weaken the intellectual demands on students in the areas of language and literature."

Finally, the Common Core national standards include college-and-career-readiness standards. President Obama's blueprint for reauthorization of ESEA says that while all states have developed and implemented their own standards, "in many cases these standards do not reflect the knowledge and skills needed for success after high school, either in further education or in a job."

The president's blueprint ties various grants for developing assessments; strengthening literacy programs; and improving science, technology, engineering, and mathematics programs to the adoption by states of common national college-and-career-readiness standards. The blueprint specifically cites the Common Core college-and-career-readiness standards and aligned tests.

Based on her evaluation of the Common Core college-and-career-readiness standards in English language arts, Professor Stotsky concluded that these standards "do not aim for a level of achievement that signifies readiness for authentic college-level work." Moreover, "They point to no more than readiness for a high school diploma." She also noted that "they are not internationally benchmarked." The result will be that states adopting the college-and-career-readiness national standards "will damage the academic integrity of both their post-secondary institutions and their high schools precisely because Common Core's standards do not strengthen the high school curriculum and cannot reduce the current amount of post-secondary remedial coursework in a legitimate way."

The standards in math also fail to prepare students for entrance into higher education. According to Professor Milgram, the standards "do not even cover all the topics that are required for admission to any of the state universities around the country, except possibly those in Arizona, since the minimal expectations at these schools are three years of mathematics, including at least two years of algebra and one of geometry."

Studies that purport to show the rigor of the Common Core standards have been methodologically flawed. For example, a study by the Oregon-based Educational Policy Improvement Center claims that the new national college-and-career-readiness standards align with state, international, and university standards. However, standards expert Wurman witheringly points out that the study tries to match apples with oranges; for example, saying that wording in a Common Core algebra standard "matches" similar wording in California's calculus standards.

"This is akin to writing a bunch of fragments on a paper," observes Wurman, "and then claiming that since most of the fragments are found among Shakespeare's works, hence that page is 'aligned' with, and 'as rigorous as' Shakespeare's works." Such methodological sleight of hand, he says, "boggles the mind."

Many in the education community recognize the shortcomings of the new national standards. Reporting on a survey of school districts, Catherine Gewertz of *Education Week* writes, "Fewer than 60 percent of [school] districts said they view the new standards as more rigorous than their states' previous guidelines. Fewer still – 55 percent in math, and 58 percent in English/language arts – said they believed the standards would improve student skills."

The bottom line, according to Douglas Holtz-Eakin, former director of the Congressional Budget Office, and Annie Hsiao, education policy director at the American Action Forum: "National standards are a bad idea. Nationalization of the wrong standards is even worse."

National Standards vs. the Constitution and Federal Law

Even if the national standards that President Obama wants to foist on the country were uniformly excellent and world class, the U.S. Constitution and federal law call into question his administration's nationalization effort.

The Constitution omits any mention of public education, thus leaving that responsibility "to the States, respectively, or to the people" under the 10th Amendment, which says that any power not enumerated in the Constitution and not prohibited by it is the province of the states and the public. Why did the Founding Fathers decide not to give any role in education to the federal government?

According to Neil Theobald and Jeffrey Bardzell of Indiana University, America's non-centralized, federal system of government is based on the Founding Fathers' unwillingness to trust central government with the supervision of people's liberties. Local people believed they knew their community and their children best. Further, they noted that "high levels of local funding for schools kept locals . . . as the primary decision-makers with regard to their children's education."

Similarly, the Education Commission of the

States, citing Terry Astuto and David Clark's writings in the *Encyclopedia of Educational Research*, has observed that education has remained the domain of state and local governments throughout most of the history of the United States for three key reasons: 1) the Founding Fathers did not trust centralized government; 2) a tradition of local control of schools has been established; and 3) until recently, persons elected to executive and legislative offices did not succeed in reversing the passive federal role in education established in the Constitution.

Nationalizing education standards and testing is exactly the type of federal scheme that goes against the intent of the Constitution and the wisdom of the nation's founders. "Why would you ever," asks Neal McCluskey, associate education director at the Washington-based Cato Institute, "want to subject the nation and its children to a federal government that has potentially unlimited power in education and could very possibly produce calamitous results for all?" Further, "why would you want to force schools and children to sit atop a constantly quaking foundation, one subjected to perpetual and potentially disastrous lurching produced by the ever-changing political desires and needs of secretaries of education, presidential administrations, congresses, and self-serving politicians of all stripes?"

The Founding Fathers certainly did not want such a situation for America's children, but because of novel interpretations of the Constitution by the courts and aggressive presidential agendas over the past five decades, the constitutional door is now open for President Obama's nationalization push. Federal statutory law, however, should also serve as a barrier to this push.

Russ Whitehurst, senior fellow in governance studies at the Brookings Institution, points out that "whereas the Education Department's [RTTT] program requires common state standards, the ARRA legislation says that the standards must be developed consistent with section 6401(e)(1)(A)(ii) of the America Competes Act, which authorizes only the support of individual states in their efforts to develop their own standards." In other words, the law says individual states must develop their own individual standards and that collective common national standards are not authorized.

The administration is also violating the ESEA/NCLB law when it requires states to adopt the national standards or some federally approved equivalent in exchange for waivers for mandated improvements in student performance. Whitehurst observes that the law grants waiver authority to the secretary of education, but it does not grant him or her "the right to impose any conditions he

---

Studies that purport to show the rigor of the Common Core standards have been methodologically flawed.

---

considers appropriate on states seeking waivers, nor is there any history of such a wholesale rewrite of federal law through use of the waiver authority."

"If you're a fan of greater presidential control of education (and domestic policy in general)," says Whitehurst, "it's celebration time." If, however, "you like the separation of powers or thought that the reauthorization of NCLB might be an opportunity to put more control of schooling into the hands of parents at the expense of district, state, and federal bureaucracies, this is not your party."

Perhaps the most consequential federal law that President Obama's nationalization agenda crosses is the prohibition against federal development of a national curriculum. Section 103b of the 1979 law that created the U.S. Department of Education clearly states, "No provision of a program administered by the Secretary or by any other officer of the Department shall be construed to authorize the Secretary or any such officer to exercise any direction, supervision, or control over the curriculum . . . of any educational institution, school, or school system." This prohibition also includes direction, supervision or control "over the selection or content of library resources, textbooks, or instructional materials by any educational institution or school system."

Opponents of the president's agenda argue that, logically, national standards will require a national test aligned with those standards and then a national curriculum aligned with those standards and tests. Such a national curriculum would violate the 1979 law. Education Secretary Duncan counters, "We have not and will not prescribe a national curriculum." The contrary actions of Duncan's department, however, speak louder than his words.

Two consortia of experts, funded by Duncan's department, are, according to Gewertz of *Education Week*, "planning to design a range of curriculum and instructional materials reflecting the common standards." A committee of the American Federation of Teachers, a key union ally of the Obama administration in the national-standards effort, urged the federal government to fund such consortia "to begin work at once on essential tools that are required to roll out the [Common Core] standards – i.e., curriculum, professional development, appropriate textbooks and other instructional materials."

Administration spokespeople have tried to distinguish between funding the development of curriculum and mandating a national curriculum. They have also tried to draw fine lines between curriculum and so-called curricular frameworks. However, these are all distinctions without a difference.

Citing the prohibitions of the 1979 law, the University of Arkansas' Jay Greene says, "I have no idea how the Department could fund the development of curriculum without also exercising some direction and supervision over that curriculum. Nor can the Department justify its current activities by claiming that they are only funding the development of curricular frameworks and instructional materials. The Department is also explicitly prohibited from directing, supervising, or controlling the content of instructional materials."

Greene also berates the obfuscation of Obama administration officials: "Their talking points clearly instruct them to 1) use curriculum as an adjective instead of a noun since 'curricular [whatever]' sounds less like 'curriculum,' 2) emphasize the plural so it sounds less uniform, 3) substitute a synonym for curriculum, such as 'framework' or 'model' so that you avoid clearly stating what you are developing."

Bill Evers, research fellow at Stanford University's Hoover Institution and a former U.S. assistant secretary of education for policy, observes, "Once the national government de-cided it was going to promote national tests, it almost perforce had to set up . . . what we call in California 'curricular frameworks,' and it had to get even into detailed lesson plans, and that's what it's doing." Just as Evers observed, Secretary Duncan praised one of the testing consortia for "developing curriculum frameworks and ways to share great lesson plans." Thus, the distinction between "curriculum" and "curricular frameworks" – or whatever terminology the administration uses – is essentially nonexistent.

"Indeed," says the Cato Institute's McCluskey, "there would be no point to the [national] standards if the intention weren't in some way to affect curricula – what is actually taught in the schools."

The Constitution omits any mention of public education, thus leaving that responsibility "to the States, respectively, or to the people" under the 10th Amendment.

Evers and several other respected academics and researchers drafted a manifesto opposing a national curriculum. When released, the manifesto, titled "Closing the Door on Innovation: Why One National Curriculum Is Bad for America," was signed by more than 100 educational and other leaders.

The manifesto, issued in May 2011, pointed out, "The two testing consortia funded by the U.S. Department of Education have already expanded their activities beyond assessment, and are currently developing national curriculum guidelines, models, and frameworks in accordance with their proposals to the Department of Education." This activity is ominous because "centralized control in the U.S. Department of Education would upset the system of checks and balances between levels of government, creating greater opportunities for special interests to use their national political leverage to distort policy."

In fact, an unholy alliance of federal government bureaucrats and Washington-based special-interest insiders has been working behind closed doors to present a nationalized education *fait accompli* to the American people.

* * *

Nationalization Empowers
Big Special Interests

One of the most disturbing practical outcomes of President Obama's master plan to nationalize standards, testing, and curriculum is the enormous advantage it gives to powerful special-interest groups based in Washington, D.C. By centralizing the standards, testing, and curriculum-making process in the nation's capital, access to this process is naturally limited to a relatively small handful of inside-the-Beltway organizations, lobbyists, advocates, and professional "experts."

Local school-board members, local principals and teachers and, most important, ordinary parents and their children are too far away and too removed from the Washington insider-information grapevine to impact the process. As Douglas Holtz-Eakin, the former CBO director, and Annie Hsiao say, "Once the feds take over, who gets to decide what the curriculum and standards look like?" Their answer: "Dense concentration of decision-making could lead to special-interest groups driving the agenda, not students."

The national teachers unions are a prime example of the inordinate influence wielded by Washington-based special interests. The American Federation of Teachers (AFT) has for years been deeply involved in the national-standards movement. In the recommendations of its committee on the rollout of the national standards, the AFT boasted that it "is a long-term supporter of higher common standards" and that "the Common Core State Standards for English language arts and math were designed with strong input by teachers and other experts." *Education Week* corroborates the AFT's braggadocio, noting, "The union's teachers were involved in the standards writing." That involvement no doubt meant that the union was able to steer the standards, at least in part, according to its ideological and self-interested goals.

The AFT's rollout document slammed the previous state-standards-based accountability systems for promoting "excessive testing and test preparation" and "narrowing of the curriculum" that focused on core subjects. Many people – including parents, individual teachers, principals, and school-board members – might strongly disagree with the AFT's biases, but their views mattered not since the AFT, not ordinary Americans, was at the national standards-writing table. Helping write the national standards, however, is just the tip of the iceberg of the union's involvement in the nationalization process.

The AFT says that it "will work with the two assessment consortia funded by the U.S. Department of Education to ensure that teachers and other educators are involved every step of the way in the design, field-testing and implementation of any new assessments." The union then uses some important code words, i.e., that the new national tests "deal with deeper thinking – not just rote memory."

Decoded, the union does not want the new national test to focus on factual knowledge, which teachers find boring to teach and which offer cut-and-dried right or wrong answers.

Instead, the union seems to favor more-amorphous progressive education concepts such as higher-order or critical-thinking skills, which Robert Ennis, author of *The Cornell Thinking Tests*, says involve "reasonable, reflective thinking that is focused on deciding what to believe and do." National tests based on such vague notions may allow for more wiggle room as to what constitutes a full-credit answer, thereby potentially improving student test scores and thus reflecting better on the teaching profession, all of which satisfies the self-interest of the AFT and its members. Parents who want a less subjective measurement of their children's knowledge and skills would be out of luck.

Besides influencing the standards and tests, the AFT is gearing up to influence the entire national-standards-implementation process, which includes the creation of curriculum aligned with the national standards. "It should be noted that the AFT," reports *Education Week*, "is working on a wide variety of materials and resources to support teachers in implementing the common [national] standards, such as model lesson plans, and is also designing a curriculum-review process to help educators and district and state officials evaluate how well various curriculum resources embody the standards."

Randi Weingarten, the head of the AFT, says, "Someone has to be out there saying, 'In order to do this, these are the things we need to do.'" The union must therefore help direct the implementation process. The union's efforts to promote its own model lesson plans and design its own curriculum-review process indicate that the brass ring for the AFT is to create a national curriculum that reflects its self-interested priorities. Despite the protestations of AFT officials that they are not seeking a single mandatory curriculum, Weingarten told an *Education Week* reporter that public education needs "common, sequential curriculum" so teachers "are not making it up every day." Such language looks and smells like a national curriculum.

What would an AFT-influenced national curriculum look like? The union's rollout

Nationalizing education standards and testing is exactly the type of federal scheme that goes against the intent of the Constitution and the wisdom of the nation's founders.

document says a curriculum should not be "prescriptive or scripted" and must allow "appropriate teacher autonomy." Yet many high-performing schools have achieved great success with scripted curriculum, such as the Open Court phonics-based reading program and the Saxon math curriculum. Indeed, one of the oft-cited problems facing many schools is their inability to rein in teachers' "do your own thing" teaching methods, even if those methods are shown not to improve student achievement. Yet powerful special interests like the AFT are perfectly positioned to shape a nationalized curriculum to their own liking, regardless of contrary evidence and the wishes of parents and their children.

Remember, the massive influence exerted by the AFT is just a single example of the power of Washington-based special interests. Add up these examples, and it is very clear that the average concerned citizen will have no power to impact the education of the next generation of Americans.

NATIONALIZATION DISEMPOWERS THE PEOPLE

The flip side of special-interest empowerment under national standards is the disempowerment of the American people. The further policymaking is seated from ordinary citizens, the less powerful and influential those citizens are. Even if the public finally finds out that the national standards, tests, and curriculum, which are financed with their hard-earned tax dollars, are deficient or objectionable, there will be precious little they will be able to do about it.

"If we discover a mistake or wish to try a new and possibly better approach," observes Professor Jay Greene, "we can't switch." Testifying before the U.S. House of Representatives Subcommittee on Early Childhood, Elementary, and Secondary Education, Greene warned, "We are stuck with whatever national choices we make for a very long time. And if we make a mistake, we will impose it on the entire country." The most affected will be parents and their children.

Writing in *The Hill's Congress Blog,* Jane Robbins, a senior fellow at the pro-parent Preserve Innocence Project, asks important questions: "And if this federalized education policy turns out to be unsatisfactory – as, given the federal government's track record on running things, it inevitably will – what recourse will parents have? Can they call their local school board, or schedule an appointment with their state legislator? What good will that do, when the problem is created within the depths of a federal bureaucracy, or even worse, by a corporation that created curricula and assessment pursuant to federal contracts that parents don't even know about?"

As seen so far, the national standards are costly, academically questionable, and deficient, contra-legal and contra-constitutional. There is more than enough reason for the public, especially parents, to want change. Yet they are unlikely to get it given the byzantine, centralized nationalization process created by the Obama administration.

In fact, because of the federal carrots and sticks used by the administration, states like Kentucky signed onto the national standards before the standards were even written or before the public was informed or notified. During the standards-creation process, the public was kept in the dark. When eighth-grade Algebra I was dropped from the national standards, Ze'ev Wurman said, "There was no discussion, no public debate." As the national standards, tests, and curricula morph over the coming years, those changes will be at the prodding of Washington insiders, not the American people.

Some proponents of the national standards argue that parents really don't have much power in the current state-based standards-and-accountability system. While admittedly, it is not easy for parents to change decisions made in their state capitals, it is still easier and more possible than trying to effect change in Washington. Take, for example, the recent battle over changes to California's social-studies curriculum.

In 2011, California Gov. Jerry Brown signed a controversial bill mandating that public K–12 social-science instruction include the study of lesbian, gay, bisexual, and transgendered (LGBT) individuals and their contributions. The law prohibits teachers from teaching anything that may adversely reflect on persons because of their LGBT orientation and places this same prohibition on instructional materials. Many parents worried about the potential politicization of education and the indoctrination of their children and decided to take action.

Parents and pro-family organizations took advantage of California's initiative process to try and place a referendum to repeal the law on the state ballot. This large-scale grassroots movement undertook the always-difficult task of collecting more than a half-million valid signatures to qualify the referendum. As it turned out, the parents came a few thousand signatures short of qualifying the referendum for a vote. Despite their loss, the effort by these parents demonstrated that there are direct avenues for an angered public to seek

---

Several Canadian provinces have taken advantage of their educational autonomy to craft broad parental-choice programs.

---

change at the state and local level that would not be available if standards, testing, and curricula were centralized at the national level.

"Like the Golden Apple or the One Ring," predicts Greg Forster, senior fellow at the Foundation for Educational Choice, "national curriculum and testing will continuously generate fresh hostility and cultural warfare as long as they exist." He then warns, "And once you forge this ring, there's no Mount Doom to drop it into."

If future presidential administrations, federal bureaucrats, and powerful special-interest groups inserted a national equivalent of the California curricular law into the national standards and curriculum, there would be few direct and effective recourses for parents.

SOLUTION: DECENTRALIZATION AND PARENTAL CHOICE

The Obama administration believes centralized national standards are essential for improving student achievement. Yet America's neighbor to the north, Canada, has no federal ministry of education and no national standards. Instead, control of education is left to the provinces. Canada also consistently outperforms the U.S. on international student-achievement tests.

On the 2009 Programme for International Student Assessment (PISA) reading exam, Canadian students scored significantly above the average of Organisation for Economic Co-operation and Development (OECD) member countries, while the U.S. scored about average. The difference was even wider on the PISA math exam, on which Canada scored above the OECD average and the U.S. scored below average.

Several Canadian provinces have taken advantage of their educational autonomy to craft broad parental-choice programs. Alberta, for instance, offers the greatest variety of choice of schools to parents in the country and also has the nation's highest test scores. Parents in Alberta can choose between public schools or religious, independent schools, both of which are publicly funded. Also, public funding, in the form of a voucher, may follow a child to charter schools and accredited private schools.

The competition spurred by giving parents a choice of schools has improved the performance of the public schools and raised the achievement of all students. In fact, Alberta's immigrant students score higher on tests than their American counterparts. Increasing numbers of American parents are calling for the same right to choose that Canadian parents have.

While there are no grassroots parent demonstrations demanding national standards, the inaugural National School Choice Week in January 2011 touched off rallies at state capitols, town-hall meetings, and other community events from coast to coast. Tens of thousands of parents and concerned citizens came together to urge policymakers to give parents the ability to choose the public or private school that best meets the needs of their children. Lawmakers in a number of states responded with new parental-choice programs.

In 2011, 12 states expanded or created parental-choice programs. The most significant of these actions came in Indiana, where Gov. Mitch Daniels signed into law the most expansive choice program in the U.S., which will provide publicly funded voucher scholarships to low- and middle-income students. Eventually, 600,000 students will be eligible for these voucher scholarships.

In her testimony to the Washington State Legislature opposing the national standards, Laurie Rogers, a parent, author, and child advocate, spoke for many parents across the country when she said, "The answer is not to give away more control – it is to regain control at local levels, and hold those local people accountable. Something needs to be done, but not this. Not the [Common Core state standards]. Not RTTT. Not the centralization and federalization of public education. Not the removal of the people's voice and our vote. We need MORE voice, more choice, and more options for parents and teachers. Competition is good for education. The CCSS/common assessments will add to costs, lower standards, eliminate choice, and ultimately not help children learn better."

CONCLUSION

Ronald Reagan once said, "I believe a case can be made that the decline in the quality of public school education began when federal aid became federal interference in education." Barack Obama's drive to centralize the key elements of education epitomizes Reagan's observation on a grand scale.

By using billions of dollars in federal funding to strong-arm states to adopt national standards of dubious quality, along with aligned national tests and curricula, the Obama administration has raised federal intrusion into education to new heights, contrary to the constitutional intent of the Founding Fathers and contrary to clear statutory language. Transferring control over the nation's classrooms to anonymous federal bureaucrats, special-interest lobbies, and insider experts will render parents and the taxpaying public powerless. Yet parents are the very ones who have the most at stake in the education of their children.

Boston Globe columnist Jeff Jacoby rightly notes, "More government control is not the cure for what ails American schools. The empowerment of parents is. No teachers' union, no school board, no secretary of education, and no president will ever love your children, or care about their schooling, as much as you do."

Barack Obama is becoming the educational equivalent of French King Louis XIV, who reputedly said, "*L'Etat, c'est moi*" ("I am the state"). Against this centralized statism, giving parents the power to choose the best school for their children is the revolution that American education truly needs.

First American edition published in 2012 by Encounter Books, an activity of Encounter for Culture and Education, Inc., a nonprofit, tax exempt corporation. Encounter Books website address: www.encounterbooks.com

Manufactured in the United States and printed on acid-free paper. The paper used in this publication meets the minimum requirements of ANSI/NISO z39.48–1992 (R 1997) (*Permanence of Paper*).

FIRST AMERICAN EDITION

LIBRARY OF CONGRESS CATALOGING-IN-PUBLICATION DATA

Izumi, Lance T., 1958–
Obama's education takeover / Lance T. Izumi.
p. cm. — (Encounter broadsides)
ISBN 978-1-59403-628-6 (pbk. : alk. paper)
ISBN 1-59403-628-4 (pbk. : alk. paper)
1. Education and state—United States. 2. Educational accountability—Government policy—United States. 3. Education—Standards—Government policy—United States. I. Title.
LC89.198 2012
379.73—dc23
2011041663

10 9 8 7 6 5 4 3 2 1